ideals VALENTINE

I like old-fashioned valentines
All trimmed in fancy lace,
With the pretty glossy figures,
Each with a handsome face.

And the messages delivered,
How stirring to the heart,
With a core of inspiration
That mortals can impart.

Oh, how delicate the feeling,
In verses so sincere,
Give the valentines a glamour
Which tends to last all year.

Anton J. Stoffle

Publisher, Patricia A. Pingry
Editor, Ramona Richards
Art Director, David Lenz
Permissions, Kathleen Gilbert
Copy Editor, Peggy Schaefer
Phototypesetter, Karen Davidson
Production Manager, Jan Johnson

ISBN 0-8249-1049-4

IDEALS—Vol. 44, No. 1 February MCMLXXXVII IDEALS (ISSN 0019-137X) is published eight times a year,
February, March, May, June, August, September, November, December
by IDEALS PUBLISHING CORPORATION, Nelson Place at Elm Hill Pike, Nashville, Tenn. 37214-8000
Second class postage paid at Nashville, Tennessee, and additional mailing offices.
Copyright © MCMLXXXVII by IDEALS PUBLISHING CORPORATION.
POSTMASTER: Send address changes to Ideals, Post Office Box 148000, Nashville, Tenn. 37214-8000
All rights reserved. Title IDEALS registered U.S. Patent Office.
Published simultaneously in Canada.

SINGLE ISSUE—$3.50
ONE-YEAR SUBSCRIPTION—eight consecutive issues as published—$15.95
TWO-YEAR SUBSCRIPTION—sixteen consecutive issues as published—$27.95
Outside U.S.A., add $4.00 per subscription year for postage and handling.

Front and back covers by H. Armstrong Roberts

Inside front cover by Gerald Koser

Inside back cover by Ed Cooper

A Walk with You

We took a walk the other day,
  Together, you and I.
We walked along a country stream
  Beneath the winter sky.

The fluffy softness of the snow
  That blew across my face
Clothed each tree and every bush
  With silvery webs of lace.

I love to do the things you do,
  To see the things you see.
I like to walk along with you
  Beneath snow-covered trees.

Bonnie Gaunt

Photo Opposite
WINTER WALK
Barbara Laatsch-Hupp

Winter Breakfast Time

Remember how it used to snow
Those winters of the long ago?
With pearly drifts up fence post high
To meet flakes whirling from the sky.

We'd wear our boots and mufflers, too,
And, laughing, somehow stumble through
The alabaster sculptures swirled
By nature in her winter world.

Inside the barn, the pleasant smells
Of corn and hay told all was well.
The bay horse nickered in his stall,
Our eager cattle waited, all
Eyes turned to us expectantly,
Then lowed and munched so thankfully.

At last when every one was fed,
We raced each other to the shed
For big armloads of hickory wood,
Then kitchen warmth so rich and good.

When Mother had the table set,
The family quietly had met.
Each loved one in his special place,
We bowed our heads to ask God's grace.

Town might have been a world away,
That snowy, ice-trimmed winter day,
But in my memory, I confess,
I've never known more happiness.

Dan A. Hoover

A Winter Haven

A tiny winter haven
That we could call our own:
Home was a cozy corner
Where no one felt alone,

Although the snow sloped downward
Like frosting on a cake
To decorate the bridges
And ice the little lake...

A lovely still came calling—
A sort of mystery—
We huddled close together
In white tranquility...

A tiny winter haven
That we could call our own:
Home was a cozy corner
Where no one felt alone.

June Masters Bacher

Photo Opposite
CRYSTALLIZED LANDSCAPE
Ken Dequaine

Editor's Note: "American Crossroads" is a regular feature of *Ideals*, presenting photographs, stories, and jokes which have been submitted by our readers, about uniquely American events or experiences. If you have a 50 to 75 word account or photograph of an unusual or interesting occurrence unique to an American lifestyle or heritage, we would like to know. Send your submission to American Crossroads, c/o Ideals Editorial, P.O. Box 141000, Nashville, TN 37214-1000. Please send only copies of manuscripts and duplicates of photographs or slides since submissions will not be returned. We will pay $10 for each printed submission. In upcoming issues we will feature articles on square dancing, unusual mailboxes, barbershop quartets, and local festivals and celebrations. This month we are featuring some unusual sculptures and the innovative artists who created them.

When many people hear the word "sculpture," they immediately think of the stone statues which grace parks and museums. In January, 1986, however, sculptors from around the world gathered in Milwaukee, Wisconsin, to work on fascinating creations in a different medium: snow.

Fourteen teams met to compete in the International Snow Sculpting Competition. The competition was hosted by WinterFun, Inc., of Milwaukee, which provided each team with a block of frozen snow 10 feet high, 10 feet long, and 10 feet wide. The sculptors had only four days to complete their creations, and they could not use internal supports or coloring agents. The results were as varied as they were beautiful, ranging from a whale emerging from the ocean to a group of people facing into the wind.

Prior to the 1986 competition, Milwaukee was chosen as the permanent site of the competition when it is held in the United States. This designation will enable the citizens of Wisconsin to witness the creation of the snowy works of art for many years to come.

Shauna Parsons
Milwaukee, Wisconsin

Photographs by Bob Brinkman

Paul Baliker, a wood sculptor from Ormond Beach, Florida, believes that there is life in wood and his job is to bring it out. A self-taught artist, he realizes that his techniques are a bit odd. He uses a chainsaw, sanders, and grinders for all the rough sculpting. Detail work is done with meticulous precision by using carving knives.

Paul uses cedar driftwood found in hideaway corners of Florida's Crystal River, and because of the twisted shapes of the wood, he can't always be in command of an idea. "Sometimes the natural shapes indicated by the wood are the cause of my ideas. At times I can see things in the driftwood before I start to carve; other times ideas flow into what is already there, then I let the pieces develop by themselves," confesses Paul.

His subjects are usually themes from nature. He works a great deal with endangered species and finds satisfaction in educating people through the messages in his work.

Joanne Kash
Holly Hill, Florida

Photograph by Joanne Kash

What do you see when you look at a pile of sand? Marc Altamar of Daytona Beach, Florida, sees life. He starts with a large pile of sand, "takes away what shouldn't be there," and creates magnificent figures on the beach.

Marc began sculpting sand in Ocean City, Maryland, when he was fifteen. His work soon became a tourist attraction, but Marc left the security of Ocean City to travel, finally settling in Daytona Beach, where he has concentrated on improving his art.

He works with loose sand, using only spray paint and acrylics for details. His sculptures are soft, like cloth, and will crumble if touched. Untouched, the beach sculptures will last for months. Marc has also carried his work indoors, creating sculptures for several Florida malls. If left undisturbed, his indoor creations will last several years.

Marc Altamar is a "Master Sandman," a gentle artist who takes an ordinary substance and makes it magnificent.

Jaime MacPherson
Nashville, Tennessee

Photograph by Joanne Kash

Valentine Treats

Strawberry and Chocolate Mousse

Yield: 4 servings

1 package (10-ounces) frozen strawberries, thawed
1 envelope unflavored gelatin
¼ cup cold water
½ cup milk
⅓ cup HERSHEY'S Cocoa
¼ cup sugar
½ teaspoon vanilla
1 cup heavy *or* whipping cream
  Fresh strawberries
  Chocolate leaves (below)

Drain strawberries, reserving 3 tablespoons of the syrup; set aside. Sprinkle gelatin onto water in blender container; let stand 5 minutes to soften. Meanwhile, heat milk in small saucepan over low heat until hot; do not boil. Add hot milk to gelatin mixture; blend on medium speed until gelatin is dissolved. Add HERSHEY'S Cocoa and sugar; blend on medium speed until sugar is dissolved. Add strawberries, reserved strawberry syrup and vanilla; blend well. Add heavy cream; blend well. Pour into 4 dessert dishes. Cover; chill several hours or overnight. Garnish with fresh strawberries and chocolate leaves.

Individual Chocolate Soufflés

Yield: 4 servings

¼ cup butter *or* margarine, softened
⅔ cup sugar
½ teaspoon vanilla
2 eggs
⅓ cup unsifted all-purpose flour
⅓ cup HERSHEY'S Cocoa
¾ teaspoon baking powder
⅓ cup milk
½ cup heavy *or* whipping cream
1 tablespoon confectioners' sugar

Grease and sugar four 5 or 6-ounce ramekins or custard cups; set aside. Cream butter or margarine, sugar and vanilla in small mixer bowl until light and fluffy. Add eggs, one at a time, beating well after each addition. Combine flour, HERSHEY'S Cocoa, and baking powder; add alternately with milk to creamed mixture. Beat 1 minute on medium speed. Divide batter evenly among prepared baking dishes. Place in 8-inch square pan; pour hot water into pan to depth of ½ inch around cups. Bake at 325° for 45 to 50 minutes or until cake tester inserted halfway between edge and center comes out clean. Remove from oven and allow to stand in water 5 minutes. Remove from water; cool slightly. Serve in baking dishes or invert into individual dessert dishes. Beat cream with confectioners' sugar until stiff; spoon onto warm soufflés.

Chocolate Leaves

Wash and thoroughly dry rose or lemon leaves. Melt HERSHEY'S Semi-Sweet or Milk Chocolate Chips in top of double boiler over hot, not boiling, water; stir until completely melted. With small soft-bristled pastry brush, brush melted chocolate on *underside* of each leaf. (The underside provides attractive markings.)

Avoid getting chocolate on the front of the leaf; it will make removal difficult. Place coated leaves on wax paper-covered cookie sheet; chill until firm.

Carefully peel the leaves away from the chocolate; do not try to peel the chocolate from the leaves. Cover; chill until ready to use.

Denim, Mud, and Chocolates

I was shopping for a few things one Valentine's Day and decided to test my wits at matching men with the boxes of candy they'd choose for their sweethearts. I strategically placed myself in an area of the store where I could unobtrusively keep an eye on the Valentine goodies.

Certain men pick certain boxes of candy—it's as simple as that. It's well worth a few moments of observation just to prove it. I have always applauded myself on my acute powers of observation of the male shopping traits during Valentine's. I can usually tell what they'll pick as soon as they enter the door of the store and head toward the candy rack.

I watched him as his big-heeled boots carried him across the floor. His long arms swung free, keeping easy pace with his slow-strided waltz that appeared to say, "I've got all day to do this, but get out of my way anyhow so I can just do it and get going."

His tall frame was covered in denim from the stretch of his wide shoulders to the muddy heels of his boots. Slightly curly hair protruded from beneath a soiled cap perched at a rather jaunty angle on his head. He was a bit rough around the edges, but neat at the same time. There was a well-worn but expensive leather knife case attached to his belt, and I thought he was probably a hunter taking a necessary break in his hunting routine along the hedgerows. I couldn't wait to see if I was right about his selection.

I gathered up my own supplies and took one final glance over the mystery man dressed in denim. For the moment, he had the entire aisle to himself. He shoved his big, rough hands into his pockets and paraded up and down the aisle in front of the candy before finally choosing one.

Nope, I thought to myself. That one's not right for you. It's too little. As if he heard what I was thinking, he replaced it and reached for another.

Still not right, I thought. It's too gaudy. This man was many things, but gaudy he was not, so I didn't think his sweetheart would be either. He apparently considered that, for he soon tossed that one aside as well and reached for the third one. I smiled. He turned the satin box over, mashing the top as he picked at the cellophane that enclosed it. He held it in his left hand while examining a more decorated one with a plastic rose and ribbon beneath the clear wrapper.

No, I thought again. You already have the one you need. Stop while you're ahead and take the one in your left hand. The box in the big man's left hand was definitely for him and his sweetheart.

Finally, he made his decision. He laid the rose-topped box down and proceeded to the cash register with the simpler but more elegant box of candy. I was right behind him by this time, more than ready to head back home as I was amply satisfied with my matchmaking on the candy aisle. He left the store while I paid for my purchases.

The cold wind had me scurrying across the parking lot toward my car with my purse and purchases hugged close to my chest. With keys in hand, I began to unlock my car. Then I noticed the big man in denim standing near the back of a pickup truck that looked as if it had been dipped in mud and oven baked.

I continued to stand there as if frozen numb from the cold, but actually out of sheer amazement and disbelief. The big man dressed in denim and wearing muddy boots peeled off the cellophane wrapper, removed the lid, and lovingly fed his elegant box of Valentine candy to his hunting dog.

Gail L. Roberson

The Valentine Box

In the village of my childhood
A one-room schoolhouse sat,
And on this day of valentines
My thoughts keep going back,
Back to that childhood setting...
Ah, once again in time
I see upon the teacher's desk
A box marked, "Valentines."

The bashful boys and bashful girls
(And those not bashful, too)
Placed sentiments into this box,
Valentines they'd choose.
Some were most original
And some were penny-bought,
But each was sent to "My Sweetheart,"
Names ranged from Ned to Maude.

In the village of my childhood
A one-room schoolhouse sat,
And on this day of valentines
I still recall the lad
That sent this lace-trimmed valentine
Tucked safely in this trunk,
And once again in childlike tones
Resounds love's old sweet song.

Loise Pinkerton Fritz

Photo Opposite
SCHOOLTIME VALENTINES
Gerald Koser

Valentine Memories

My Valentine's Day memories date back to the little one-room school that I attended as a little girl. Valentine parties there were truly delightful, as we were enveloped in a fantasyland made out of valentines, delectable heart-shaped tarts, pink-frosted cupcakes decorated with tiny red hearts, cherry-flavored drink, and heart-shaped candies with little verses on them.

The memories implanted by those early Valentine's Days have remained; I never cease to look forward with joy and anticipation to another Valentine's Day. Cards are chosen with great care and go off in the mail to loved ones. Heart-shaped, red or pink satin pillows trimmed with delicate white lace, or maybe pink and white gingham ones, are handmade, then gently wrapped in tissue paper and trimmed with a lovely red satin or velvet bow—thoughtful gifts that warm the heart and say, "I love you." Some of the happiest memories include the times I remembered someone who didn't expect a Valentine gift. Flowers, homemade fudge, delicate cupcakes, or maybe a plant are thoughtful ways of lighting up the world for giver and recipient.

I love gifts and the holidays which inspire them. Living on a farm

means living by the calendar, and we wait for holidays with great expectations. Holidays seem to make the farm world go around a bit smoother. My heart is lifted as I watch young folks enjoying the holidays as much as I do, especially St. Valentine's Day. Parties at churches, grange halls, and schools are as pleasurable today as they were when I was much younger, and spreading love is more important than ever in the world we live in today.

On Valentine's Day, the world glows with expressions of love which radiate joy and happiness. "I love you" are the most wonderful words in the world and should be an inspiration to us all. They certainly inspired my most treasured Valentine's gift—a red, heart-shaped valentine that my grandson made for me in nursery school. He proudly presented it to me, and his eyes twinkled merrily as the large red paper heart was placed on the kitchen wall for all to see. His gift is a constant reminder of all the little hands which have given lovingly handmade valentines—the chubby, dimpled hands of my children and grandchildren—and the tiny hands which I extended to my mother so long ago, excitedly giving her a valentine to say, "I love you!"

Helen Colwell Oakley

Snow

Snowflakes on the hemlocks
Glisten in the sun,
And the birdbath's covered
Like a sugar-coated bun.

A fairy wand's been waving
Across our world of gray,
Creating things of beauty
For this, a brand new day.

Hills and fields are blanketed
With snow so pure and white;
A fairyland has been revealed
With visions of delight.

Children gay with laughter
Are wading through the snow,
Making forts and snowmen
As they scurry to and fro.

But now, the day is ended,
And cool the frosty night;
Children all are homeward bound
With eyes and cheeks still bright.

Tiny ones are tuckered out
And in their soft warm beds,
Each receiving Mother's kiss
As their prayers are said.

In their dreams they're wafting
Toward another day—
With visions of more happiness
As in the snow they'll play.

Bernice Schulze

Photo Opposite
WINTER CREATION
H. Armstrong Roberts

First Grade Valentines

February snow
   falls outside my classroom window.

Winter winds
   whip and whirl it,
      making tiny Christmas-card drifts
      in the corners of the windowpanes.

My first-graders sit
   restlessly doing seat work.
Anxious eyes steal secret glances
   at the paper-heart-covered door.

Brown bags,
   decorated with crudely cut hearts
      of red, pink, white,
   line the chalk trays.

Room mothers
   magically appear,
      laden with gallons of red punch,
      balancing boxes of cupcakes
         sprinkled with chocolate hearts.

The reading table is transformed
   with a red paper cloth and a
      fold-out centerpiece.

Small hands reach up,
   expectant, eager
as I pass out the
   valentine bags.

Stubby fingers feel envelopes,
   opening fat ones first,
   knowing these contain

flat red suckers,
penny candy,
fistfuls of red-hots.

The room resounds
   with the chaotic chorus of children's voices.
"What does this say, Teacher?"
"Hey, there's no name inside.
   Who's this one from?"
"My name is spelled with two t's."
"I didn't get a valentine from Jay
   and I gave him my nicest one!"

I open the valentines
   piled on my desk.
Ten of them are identical.
Three contain hankies
   with embroidered hearts in the corners.
One is handmade
   of white lace doilies.
   I LOVE YOU is printed
      in bold red crayon.

Thank you, God,
   for Valentine's Day,
   for a day of unabashed
      I Love You.

And someday, Lord,
   when my students experience
   the frustration and wonder of adolescence,
let them remember today
when love was
   as simple as dime-store valentines,
   as tangible as chocolate cupcakes.

Mary Lou Carney

A Boy and His Dog

A boy and his dog seem to share
Abiding love beyond compare;
A certain look on a little boy's face
Can make a puppy slow his pace.

The boy and dog both understand
Which one should have the upper hand,
But with a puppy's loving glance,
The master hasn't got a chance.

A dog asks little and gives so much
And says a lot with a friendly touch
To let you know he's standing by
In case he's needed by a guy!

A faithful-trusty, loyal friend
And so remains until the end
And sees no need to fret or whine,
He thinks a dog's life mighty fine.

Laurie E. Wilcox

They romp together on the lawn
With stick or ball or toy,
A barking, jumping puppy
And a freckle-faced small boy.

They go down toward the riverbank
And while away an hour,
Or climb the hill to "Pirate's Cave"
And far horizons scour.

Perhaps they lie in the clover patch
To scan the sky for planes
Or go into the basement
To build models when it rains.

They have an understanding
That's quite wonderful to see,
Whatever the little master decides,
The puppy does agree.

Shirley Sallay

A Girl and Her Kitten

A little girl with a kitten
Held close in her arms
Makes a pretty picture
Of a little girl's charm.

Sometimes they share a muffin
At a tea party for two.
Or kitty rides in dolly's carriage,
Wears dolly's bonnet, too.

It matters not the time or place,
If skies are gray or blue,
Companions from the very first,
The dearest friends, these two.

A little girl and a kitten
Held close in her arms
Is a precious childhood portrait
Of a little girl's tender charm!

Kay Hoffman

A little ball of fur and fluff
I'd like to call my own,
She's just a kitten with charm enough
To melt a heart of stone;
With eyes as green as new spring grass,
A nose as black as night,
A furry tail that's much in doubt
To wiggle left or right.

She isn't any special breed,
But she's a regal queen,
With tolerance and fortitude,
The like I've never seen.
She has a brand of beauty
That belongs to her alone,
This white and taffy colored kit
I'd love to call my own.

Lorraine Good

BEST FRIENDS
Photos by Robert C. Hayes

ABCDEFGHIJKLMN
OP2RSTUVWXYZóü 123
1234567890 principles

The Kiss

He hung his head, the little boy
Who had scarcely turned six.
He was shy, but so in love,
And in an awful fix.

He wanted so to show his love
To the pretty teacher there.
He loved her blue eyes, just like Mom's;
He loved her dark red hair.

He stood aloof, his heart astir;
He had nothing to bring
To the teacher, that was his,
To make his young heart sing.

With paper and a crayon red,
He had worked at home that night
Until a lovely valentine
Appeared before his sight.

a b c d e f g h i j k l m n o p q r s t u v w x y z i í ǐ i̊ l principles

"I love you," he scrawled in pen;
He signed the message, "Tom."
He held it behind his back one day
'Till all the kids were gone.

His face glowed like his own red hair;
"I brought you something. Here!"
He said, and handed her the card,
And grinned from ear to ear.

The teacher, like his mother, smiled
And praised the little lad.
He was delighted in her joy;
His heart beat wild and glad.

"I love you, too, dear little Tom,
You fill my life with bliss."
She reached into her top desk drawer,
Pulled out a chocolate kiss.

He beheld the precious gift,
A token, sweet with love.
As he unwrapped the silver foil,
God smiled down from above.

It, indeed, was his first kiss
From anyone but Mom.
How happy was the little boy,
The little boy named Tom.

Mary J. Kellar

Sharing

John Slobodnik

Give me a friend and a wood stove
And a couple of chairs nearby
When the wind is bold and the day is cold
And the clouds are thick and high.

Give me a pile of hickory logs
To keep the fire aglow,
To warm our hearts and our memories
As into the past we go.

What more could one ask than a wood fire
And a friend that is staunch and true—
One who laughs when you laugh,
And in trouble, will see you through.

Once more we play with our dolls
And set a lovely table for tea;
And guests of distinction and honor
Will visit with you and with me.

Again we remember the creek where we swam,
And in memory we can hear
The liquid lip of the babbling brook
Each time as we drew near.

Far from the house—it was quite a walk
Through fields of growing corn—
A treat for the gods was its water cool
On a hot and dusty morn.

We see the rail fence we climbed over;
The weeds were as tall as I.
And a gorgeous spider spun his web
To catch a passing fly.

The hickory logs are burning low;
The embers are losing their glow.
But we have traveled many a mile
As into the past we did go.

Just give me a friend and a couple of chairs
And a wood fire all aglow.
It's the simple things in life that count;
They grow and grow and grow!

Ina Englert

A Sermon in the Snow

New-fallen snow reminds me
Of when I was a lad,
And when the well was gettin' low
It used to worry Dad.
But Grandma said, "Now don't you fret,
We'll melt and strain the snow—
It's good enough for washin' clothes
And takin' baths, you know."
I thought that Gram was silly
'Cause the way it looked to me,
That fluffy, white, new-fallen snow
Was clean as it could be.
So Grandma had me fill a pail
And set it on the stove;
She said, "When it has melted,
You'll see—the dirt will show."
I watched it melt and shook my head,
It sure did puzzle me—
How there could be one speck of dirt
Was more than I could see.
And then she slowly poured it
Through a cloth so clean and white,
And when I saw the dirt it left,
I knew that she was right.
And Grandma said, "It's like that
As you go through life, my son,
You'll maybe think you've covered up
The little wrongs you've done;
But don't forget, though you have fooled
The folks next door to you,
That God looks right into your heart
And sees the bad you do."

How I recall Grandmother's words
Each time I watch it snow;
No matter how we hide the truth,
There's always one who'll know.

Luceille B. Carey
Batavia, New York

Winter Retreat

Clear, crisp mountain air:
Breath of God.

Torrents tumbling,
Cascading crescendo:
Praise and proclamation.

Sculptured rocks,
Tall timbered hills,
Elk and deer feeding,
Shadows, rich earth tones:
Grandeur of God.

Falls breaking
Through the frozen
Mountainside:
Faith,
Everlasting water.

Crystalline flakes
Enwrapping the earth:
God's benediction,
Mantle of love.

Nellie Savicki
Auburn, Washington

Reflections

She Comes like Morning Sunshine

(For Shirley, who made the past 19 years wonderful)

Blessed

Sometimes I sit and wonder
  How funny life would be;
If I were not blessed with you,
  How lonely I would be.

I know it's you who makes my day
  And every dream come true.
You make me laugh;
  You make me glad you're you.

I could not think how life would be
  Without you by my side.
You are everything in the world to me;
  For you I would even die.

I thank the Lord every night
  For sending you to me;
For if I were not blessed with you,
  How lonely I would be.

Peggy Highfield
Claymont, Delaware

She comes like morning sunshine
  through the windows of my life
And shines upon the carousel
  we share as man and wife.
She blossoms gently like a rose
  in the gardens of my heart
To fill my life with beauty
  that only love imparts.
She sparkles like a diamond
  throughout my darkest night
And wakes me when it's over
  with love that's warm and bright.
She's like a breath of springtime
  in my winter of discontent—
A flesh and blood valentine
  that must be heaven sent.
She comes like morning sunshine
  to answer every prayer,
And I'm forever grateful
  for each memory we share.

Clay Harrison
Tampa, Florida

Editor's Note: Readers are invited to submit unpublished, original poetry, short anecdotes, and humorous reflections on life for possible publication in future *Ideals* issues. Please send copies only; manuscripts will not be returned. Writers will receive $10 for each published submission. Send materials to "Readers' Reflections," Ideals Publishing Corporation, Nelson Place at Elm Hill Pike, Nashville, Tennessee 37214.

February Frost

Hoary frost caterpillars snuggle tight
on bare-boned trees,
dozing in the warmth
of February's promise.
Then, quiet, like a summer Sunday noon,
they wriggle free
and evaporate into gossamer,
brushing pale cheeks and kissing eyelids
with wings of hope.

Cheryl Nicklin
Regina, Saskatchewan

Swan Lake: The Classic That Failed

The forest is quiet as light from the midnight moon reflects off the still waters of a lake and casts eerie shadows in the surrounding mist. A young prince, exhausted from a long day of hunting, pauses near the lake. He had been following a flock of wild swans, but had lost them. As he turns to leave, he sees a movement and is astonished to see a woman emerge from the mist. She is the most beautiful woman he has ever seen—an ethereal creature of the magical night, adorned in soft white cloth and swan feathers. On her head is a diamond-tipped crown.

She is the Swan Queen, and this scene is from Act II of the world's most popular classical ballet, *Swan Lake*. The ballet is a story of love and magic, betrayal and forgiveness. The enduring love of the Swan Queen and Prince Siegfried has captured the imagination of every child who dreams of dancing. If there had not been a revived interest in the music of the composer during the year following his death, however, this beautiful ballet might never have reached modern audiences.

In the spring of 1875, the director of the Bolshoi Theatre, V.P. Begitchev, co-wrote a libretto with Vasily Geltzer called "The Lake of the Swan." He commissioned Peter Tchaikovsky to write the music to a ballet they hoped would become a standard in every ballet company's repertoire.

The hope faltered when the ballet was given to a second-rate ballet master who did not have the skill to choreograph the complex music of Tchaikovsky's score. He substituted familiar music and choreography from other ballets for many of Tchaikovsky's more complicated passages, and badly choreographed others. The four-act ballet was first performed in March 1877. Although it was received fairly well by

the audience, the ballet was considered an artistic failure and was removed from the Bolshoi's repertoire in 1883 after only thirty-three performances in eight years.

Peter Tchaikovsky never saw the ballet performed again; he died in 1893, believing *Swan Lake* to be a total failure. Lev Ivanov and Marius Petipa of the Maryinsky (now the Kirov) Theatre had different ideas. Tchaikovsky's death spurred a renewed

The young prince drew his crossbow and took aim at the golden-crowned swan, but his eyes clouded with tears. He dropped his bow. Never had he seen such beauty.

from *Swan Lake,* adapted from the ballet by Pamela Kennedy, illustrated by Russ Flint, copyright © 1986 by Ideals Publishing, Nashville, Tennessee.

interest in his music, and the Maryinsky choreographers revived the second act of *Swan Lake,* restoring Tchaikovsky's original music. Ivanov restaged the act for a performance during an evening of excerpts from all of Tchaikovsky's works. The performance of the act was so well received that Petipa and Ivanov decided to restore the music that had been removed and rechoreograph the entire ballet.

The completed revision of *Swan Lake* was first performed on February 8, 1895, and it is the Ivanov/Petipa choreography that has been performed by the greatest dancers of the past century. The artistic failure of 1877 was saved by two masters of the ballet, who have passed to modern audiences a creation as ethereal and magical as its heroine—a timeless story which stirs the imagination of every dreamer.

Ramona Richards

R.F.D.

The mail truck stopped, then rumbled on.
I waited 'til I knew he'd gone
Around the bend and out of sight,
Before I'd let my heart take flight.
A stillness filled the morning air,
With expectation everywhere.
The birds had stopped their songs to see
The eagerness that glowed in me.
A busy squirrel paused on his way
Across the lawn, as if to say,
"What is so special in the mail?"
He cocked his head and shook his tail.
I tried to walk a little slower,
For I knew my eagerness must show;
And so would my disappointment, too,
If there was nothing there from you.
But inside the mailbox I could see
An envelope, addressed to me
From you, all filled with loving words
That hushed the morning songs of birds.

Joan Harlow

Today's Mail

Today, I got a special letter
Just for me and penned so fine;
The message came through loud and clear
That you wrote between each line.

The written word was gay and newsy
And told of your trip in part,
But between those hand-penned lines,
You told of love to fill my heart.

The envelope was very plain;
The upper corner said "Guess Who."
I knew at once it would contain
That dearest message just from you.

So hurry home where I will wait
To greet you in our own confines,
And I will hear you say to me
What you wrote between the lines.

Minnie Frese

I'd like to give
this heart of mine
To my best, best,
best VALENTINE.

Old-Fashioned

I like old-fashioned valentines
With lots and lots of lace...
A shy boy in blue knickers and
A girl with doll-like face.

I like the old inscriptions, like
"Be mine, my valentine."
I like old-fashioned valentines;
There's love in every line.

And each one has a cupid tucked
Away somewhere, you see;
They've done it for so many years...
Dates to antiquity.

I like old-fashioned valentines!
They seem so warm and true,
And anyway, I guess I am
A bit old-fashioned, too!

Georgia B. Adams

Photos by Joanne Kash
Valentines from the collection
of Sue Lofaro

Valentines

I love old-fashioned valentines
Where ribbons, bits of lace,
And just the proper sentiment
Are blended into place.

I love the pictures they portray
Of children neatly dressed
And cupids scattered all about
To add a bit of zest.

I love the fold-out valentines
They sent long years ago,
Where scene on scene could there
   unfold
To form a lovely show.

But the favorite of my valentines
I'd have to term as new.
I opened it just yesterday,
And, dear, it came from you.

Craig Sathoff

Love

I know I heard it coming
Amid my busy way,
I heard it in the laughter
Of children at their play.

The happy song a bluebird
Sang in the honey vine.
The merry chirp of crickets,
Soft breezes in the pine
That leans beside my doorway.
The growing sounds of spring
Were magnified with wonder,
More than a spring could bring.

There was a certain something
To set the day apart;
Love nudged me on the shoulder,
Love touched me in the heart!

Jessie Cannon Eldridge

Friendly Silence

Love is a friendly silence
That travels here and there;
It shows its face in every place
Where people seem to care.

Love never boasts or vaunts itself,
Is patient, suffers long;
Then surfaces with one soft word
Or in a sudden song.
Always great, love is humble,
Forgiving, and is kind,
And when rebuffed or criticized,
Love does not seem to mind.

Sometimes it has no voice at all,
So silent is its prayer;
Then friendly hands reach out to help
And tell me love is there.

June Masters Bacher

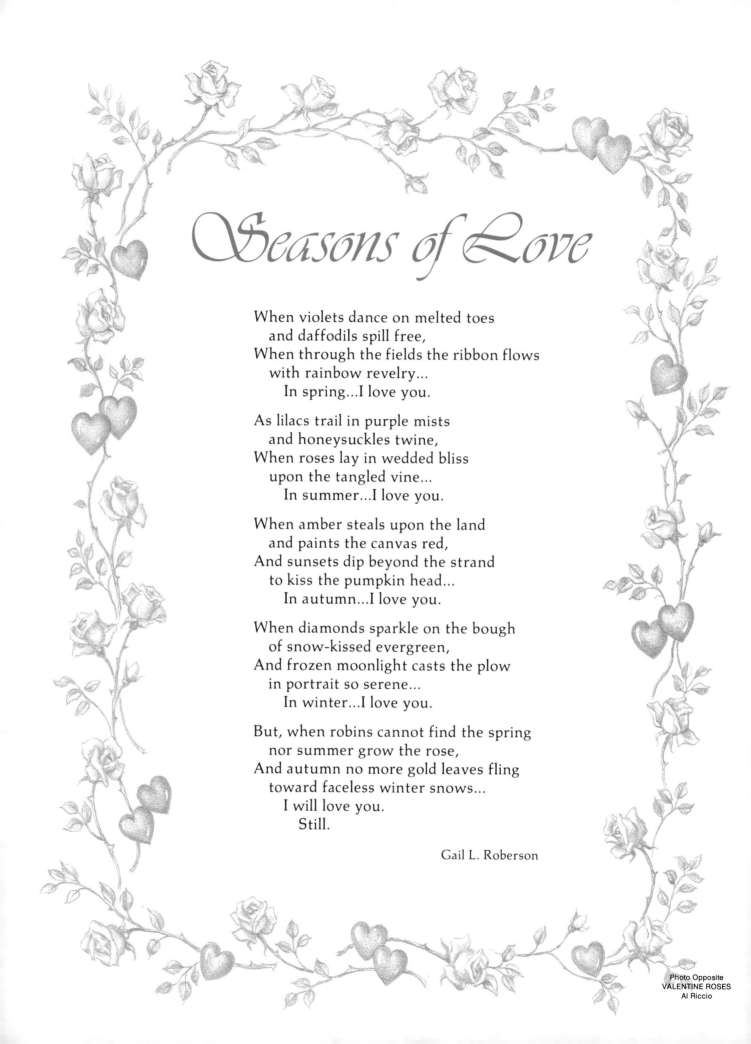

Seasons of Love

When violets dance on melted toes
 and daffodils spill free,
When through the fields the ribbon flows
 with rainbow revelry...
 In spring...I love you.

As lilacs trail in purple mists
 and honeysuckles twine,
When roses lay in wedded bliss
 upon the tangled vine...
 In summer...I love you.

When amber steals upon the land
 and paints the canvas red,
And sunsets dip beyond the strand
 to kiss the pumpkin head...
 In autumn...I love you.

When diamonds sparkle on the bough
 of snow-kissed evergreen,
And frozen moonlight casts the plow
 in portrait so serene...
 In winter...I love you.

But, when robins cannot find the spring
 nor summer grow the rose,
And autumn no more gold leaves fling
 toward faceless winter snows...
 I will love you.
 Still.

Gail L. Roberson

Photo Opposite
VALENTINE ROSES
Al Riccio

Silent Joy

When snow is softly falling
And northern winds do blow,
I like to curl in my favorite chair
Beside the fire's glow.
There to find contentment
And dream a dream or two,
While my knitting needles are busy
With yarn of varied hue.
The rhythmic click is soothing;
Cares gently fade away.
And only happy memories
Bring thoughts of yesterday.
Some folks long for summer,
With her blossoms sweet and gay;
Yet, give to me the silence
Of a snow-crowned winter day.

Shirley Sallay

Fireside Seat

Give me a cozy corner
With a comfy sofa seat,
A thrilling book within my hands,
And rest for my weary feet.

Give me a furry kitten
Snuggled up close to my side,
With a lazy peaceful purring,
And I'm fully satisfied.

Give me a glowing, burning fire
With flames that crackle and roar,
Tiny golden dancing sparks;
How could I ask for more?

Ruth H. Underhill

Midst Frills and Hearts

Midst frills and hearts and dainty lace
I take a noble stand
Because I will employ them all
To win your lovely hand.

I'll tell you of my earnest love
And what you mean to me.
(As if by now you didn't know,
As if you couldn't see!)

I'll wish you, dearest valentine,
A very happy day
With everything most wonderful
Coming all your way.

I love you, dear, and I can see
Love mirrored in your face;
I take a noble stand amidst
The hearts and bits of lace!

Georgia B. Adams

Why February 14th?

We know that Valentine's Day is February 14th, but why that date instead of March 10th or May 15th? Legends about valentines are fascinating because of their antiquity and sentimentality.

One of the most popular is the story of St. Valentine, who chose to be executed rather than renounce his faith in God. Valentinus was a young priest who was arrested by the Roman emperor, Claudius II, for helping fellow Christians escape persecution. While he was imprisoned, the blind daughter of the jailer brought him food, delivered messages, and comforted him as best she could. Although Valentinus' crime was considered serious, Claudius offered the priest his freedom if he would denounce Christianity. Not only did Valentinus refuse, but he tried to convert the pagan king, which so outraged Claudius, he ordered the priest to be stoned to death.

As Valentinus awaited his execution day, he restored the sight of the jailer's daughter who had helped him. She and her father were converted to Christianity by the miracle the priest had wrought. On the eve of his death, Valentinus wrote a farewell note to the girl thanking her for all the kindness she had shown him and signed it, "From your Valentine." The next day a messenger delivered the note and a bouquet of violets to the girl at the exact moment of Valentinus' death. The day was February 14, A.D. 270.

Another legend has it that the Romans celebrated February 14th as the day the birds chose their mates—and the Romans linked that courtship with the courtship of their own young people.

The date also marked the pagan feast of Lupercalia in ancient Rome, when the names of girls were drawn by lot. The boys who drew them courted the girls for a year. If the couples weren't married by the end of the year, they started all over again with new partners when the feast was again celebrated on February 14th.

According to another legend, the first valentine ever sent was delivered to the wife of Charles, Duke of Orleans, when he was imprisoned in the Tower of London in 1415. That valentine is in the British Museum.

All these legends indicate that "Be my valentine" has been said and written for centuries more than "Merry Christmas." (Christmas cards were not exchanged much before the mid-nineteenth century.) Valentines have been exchanged since the fourteenth century, although they didn't make their appearance in the United States until the mid-nineteenth century.

The golden age of valentines in America was created by Esther Howland, the daughter of a stationer in Worcester, Massachusetts, who graduated from Mount Holyoke in 1847 and returned home to live as a proper Victorian lady. Almost by accident, however, she became a prosperous businesswoman.

On Valentine's Day, a year after Esther's graduation, she received an elegant valentine that delighted her so much she decided to send her own valentines the following year. Her father ordered cut-outs, lace-paper blanks, paper flowers, and stick-ons with expensive envelopes from London. Esther created such stunning valentines that her brother, a salesman for the family firm, showed them to a number of his customers. The valentines were a hit, and he returned home with orders totaling more than $5,000.

Impressed with his daughter's success, Mr. Howland ordered great quantities of materials and set up a workroom in the home for Esther's valentine factory. She set up an assembly-line procedure employing young ladies to perform the various tasks involved in compiling the valentines.

By 1850, Esther's valentines were the rage of New England, and she became known as the Valentine Queen of America. Her valentines sold for as much as $35.00. Esther reigned as queen until 1870 when the one-of-a-kind valentine was threatened by mass production. In 1881, George C. Whitney bought Esther's business and continued manufacturing lovely and expensive valentines. Although he continued his business until 1942, competition had driven the price of valentines down to as little as a nickel, with none selling for more than $5.00. Today valentines outnumber all other cards bought for special occasions and holidays. Who receives the most valentines?

Sweethearts? Wrong! *Mothers* receive three times as many valentines as sweethearts. And if that isn't heart-rending enough, *teachers* receive more than mothers. In fact, just about everyone receives more valentines than lovers.

Now that you know why valentines are exchanged on the 14th of February, the exchange of valentines this year should be even more fun and meaningful.

Vivian Buchan

My All for You

If you could know the part you play
In all I try to be,
You would begin to understand
How much you mean to me.

And you would know that everything
I ever undertake
Is not for my convenience but
For your beloved sake.

That I am happy only when
I know that what I do
Will ultimately bring about
Some happiness for you.

I never see the sun begin
Or end another day
Without I say a silent prayer
To help you on your way.

You mean so much to me that I
Must honestly confess
That everything I ever do
Is for your happiness.

James J. Metcalfe

Photo Opposite
MEMORY ROSES
Barry Runk
Grant Heilman Photography

drawn

light's erful dawn;

things gay,

ay-ti aylay.

shape

an t

view

Her

it

did m

omises as sweet;

ure ot too h t or good

man re, ly food,

or transien s, simple wiles,

ise tears, and

l n serene

machine;

ughtful brea

My Shining Knight

My "knight in shining armor"
  drives a red pickup,
  wears flannel shirts,
    and flaunts a ragged baseball cap
      instead of a plume.

He brings me lilac bouquets,
  not long-stem roses.
Sonnets aren't his style,
  but he has the most eloquent eyes.

And I'm his "damsel in distress"
 whenever the kitchen sink clogs,
        my car won't start,
        the baby has colic—again.

He romps with our kids,
  picks up his dirty socks,
  holds me when I'm blue,
    and still calls me "Honey."

He lets me cry at movies,
        befriend stray cats,
        sleep in on Saturday mornings.

He fights fierce dragons—
  INFLATION, UNEMPLOYMENT—
and emerges with the spring
  still in his step.

He is my lover,
    my provider,
        my husband—

who helps me through
  Mondays and
    other traumas.

                    Mary Lou Carney

Forever Valentine

I love your pretty valentines,
Red paper hearts with lace.
But the heart you give me every day
Will always hold first place.

"I Love You," inscribed in gold,
Has meaning sweet and true,
But it can never mean as much
Unless it's said by you.

I'll store the paper hearts away
That time will tear apart,
But keep three words, "I Love You,"
Forever in my heart.

Elveria Blust

Photo Opposite
SWEETHEART BOUQUET
Barry L. Runk
Grant Heilman Photography

Just Being Together

There is a sacredness in being old
In fair or stormy weather,
Just dreaming of the days long past
And sweetness of being together.

There's sereneness in the evenings
As lights are softly lit;
We glory in past memories
As by the open fire we sit.

We smile and nod in comfort
With never a doubt or fear;
There's love past understanding,
With comfort of being near.

No need for words or music;
Thankful for gifts like this,
Two hearts of understanding
In holy wedded bliss.

Sacred sweetness of two hearts
In fair or stormy weather,
Sharing a lifetime harvest
And thankful of being together.

Mamie Ozburn Odum

A Valentine For You

This valentine I send to you
Is not done up in lace;
It has no flowered border
Nor a cupid on its face.
It isn't tied with ribbons
In little bows of blue;
It doesn't smell of lilacs
And it isn't even new!

But it is full of loving thoughts
For only you alone,
Recalling tender yesterdays
That you and I have known.
I have wanted so to tell you
Many times before today,
Of the sweetness you have added
To the miles along the way.

For the meadows grow the greener
As we wander hand in hand;
You have made my life a heaven
And the world a promised land.
Two lives closely joined together,
Such as we may never part!
For your valentine, my darling,
I am sending you my *heart!*

Grace E. Easley

Sufficiency

I do not dream of luxury
Or search for hidden gold,
For I have wealth beyond compare,
More than my heart can hold.

I have the eyes to realize
The beauty of God's earth—
The golden sun, the silver moon,
And other things of worth.

I have the ears to listen to
The music of the birds,
Or when a good friend speaks to me
In soft and kindly words.

But most of all I have the love
Of someone sweet and dear,
Who by my side still shares a love
That's constant year after year.

Carice Williams

Beside Me

You walk beside me every day
In everything I do
To help me with the many tasks
That make our dreams come true.

You do not walk ahead of me,
So anxious for success
That you outdistance hopes and goals
We've set for happiness.

But neither do you walk behind
While I go on ahead
To search horizons far or near
Without your strength and stead.

Your love and trust joined firm with mine,
You walk with me each day,
So that together we can share
Each joy that comes our way.

Craig Sathoff

Fingerprints of Time

Little scraps of lacy paper
Tied with a ribbon bow,
Little rhyming lines written
In the days of long ago.

Frilly laces and scenes
Of old gardens in bloom,
A little valley church,
And a bride and a groom.

A pretty linen handkerchief
And a sachet still sweet,
Folded with the old cards,
So careful and neat.

A whisp of golden tresses
Tied with a silken thread,
Some pieces of gay ribbon,
White, lavender, and red.

There is one for Mother,
And another for sister Sue—
Old-fashioned climbing roses
On a background of blue.

Little cards of lacy paper,
Each with a special line,
Racing in a rhyming caper
On yesterday's valentine.

Frilly laces and old scenes,
Every one with a rhyme,
Little bits of old ribbon,
Gay fingerprints of time!

G.W. Goretzke

Photo Opposite
YESTERDAY'S VALENTINES
Gerald Koser

Love Stages

In early February, when florists and confectioners begin to entice would-be sweethearts with their wares, my mind wanders back through the years to Valentine's Days long past. Cards, candy hearts, and bouquets of roses laced with baby's breath are beautiful, yet not nearly so eloquent as the "I love you's" traced through the stages of my life, for each age, it seems, has its own peculiar expressions of love.

I remember wrinkled, grubby notes, passed secretly despite the ever-watchful eyes of Mrs. Bryant—keeper of second grade secrets. There were misspelled sentiments scrawled with sweaty pencils and tucked inside a sweater pocket to keep company with lucky pennies and a clear green marble. What could say "I love you" better than these? I recall a secret smile, a freckled blush, devotion expressed over a shared cookie still warm from the oven.

All these attested to the reality of first love.

When hopscotch, kites, and marbles lost their places to makeup, clothes, and coiffures, "I love you's" changed as well. Whispered conversations, tentatively clasped hands, glances full of meaning—all the subtleties of teenage romance—came into play. Emotions rose and fell with a gesture or a word. He loves me, loves me not became the liturgy of youth. How bittersweet were those first romances, bright and burning, fleeting as a falling star, beautiful for a moment, then quickly gone.

With higher education came higher forms of love, or so we thought. All-night discussions over steaming cups of coffee, analytical conversations dissecting Camus, Thoreau, or Sartre. True love transcended the mundane; shared thoughts, ambitions, motivations, philosophies, these were the roots of true devotion. You said

"I love you" with a slim and gilt-bound book of poetry, and I responded with an autographed first edition. Idealism lifted us to lofty heights and love was like an ever-changing rainbow, glimmering in our eyes.

Wedding bells and satin, Mendelssohn and Bach finalized our statement of love, blending the idealism and reality. Those simple vows seemed complete, and what could say "I love you" more than the clear and honest shining of our eyes? We thought it was the completion of our love. How little we understood then, for love was just beginning; it was only an infant, waiting to grow up.

The years rolled by in never-ending cycles. As they passed, we found how many ways there were to say "I love you." Holding hands, watching our first son be born, then the second, and the third. "Let me rock the baby tonight while you sleep." "Yes, I remembered to pick up the medicine." "You go ahead, I'll watch the children today." "Surprise! I brought home dinner!" "Don't worry about the sink. I already

fixed it." How far we had traveled from Thoreau and Sartre. Yet, our love was never stronger or more intense.

Then new stages, different stages tried our love. When the children left and emptiness could have crept into the corners of our hearts, love expanded and filled the lonely places. How special are a quiet walk, a hand to hold, a smile that says "no words are needed." These all are treasures of the golden days and months we share. The fire never dies, but only glows more brightly as we enjoy its warmth.

We've traveled far, one love-stage following another like the seasons revolving in an ever-widening spiral. In the language of love, there is a constantly expanding vocabulary, new words and ways to say "I love you." This Valentine's Day instead of the hearts and flowers, sweets and sentiments of tradition, let's find fresh expressions of our love, expressions well-suited to the love-stages of today; "I love you's" meant for now—unfolding like the bright new spring that lies before us.

Pamela Kennedy

The Heart Remembers

The heart remembers the springtime of life
When love was very young,
When days were filled with candy-sweet talk
And nights were filled with song.

The heart remembers the summer of life
When love was sweet and pure,
When the world was filled with flowery days
And dreams seemed very sure.

The heart remembers the autumn of life
When love grew dearer still,
When flowers changed to colors of gold
On marriage's sacred hill.

The heart remembers in winter of life
The love that once was young,
And there in the beauty of fading days
Still sings love's old sweet song.

Loise Pinkerton Fritz

Photo Opposite
FLOWERS FOR MY LOVE
Al Riccio

Country Chronicle

Each year on Valentine's Day, Lucile and I turn hand in hand to the hills for our messages of love. February can often bring the coldest days and the deepest snows of winter; but it is also the shortest month, and soon the earth will begin to warm. February is a month whose frozen fingers of snow reach toward the more tender fingers of the spring sun. The two will meet, touch, and the warmth will start the snow melting and send the water running down the slopes in splashing songs. The sun and snow will play on our heart-strings just as purling waters play on stones in winding upland streams. The wind may still whip the snow into drifts behind stone walls and hedges, over ridges of furrows left by last fall's plow, over stubble fields, and behind the picket fence where leafless lilacs stand stark against the cold, but the sun lingers longer on the hills, steadily warming the earth.

Out here in the country, we have learned that love can be embellished by the embracing arms of the outdoor world around us. They draw and keep us near. We let the snow and sun of February stitch the embroidery of lace for our valentines. We let the miniature tracks of tree sparrows and juncos be our signatures. The winter call of chickadees and the song of finches are our words of endearment, and the reddening spires of osiers on the edge of the swampland depict the hues of our hearts.

Out of the sun and snow, Lucile and I pluck the loveliest of jewels to be worn forever in a bond of love, for out of these February hours we sculpt our valentines.

Lansing Christman

Winter Reverie

There were winter nights when the air was still
And sleigh bells rang o'er the moon-bathed hills;
When house lights shone with a golden glow,
And red barns drowsed in a world of snow.

They were wondrous nights
   that were cold and clear,
And I live them still when the snows appear;
When the air is chill and my fireside's bright
With the warmth and cheer of a winter's night.

I remember when as a lad I'd go
To a lofty hill, where the world below
Glittered and sparkled to please the eye
In the light of stars in a silent sky;

Where lanterns bobbed
   in an ice-locked vale
Like the witch's gems of a fairy tale;
And the drifting snows, like reefs of pea[r]
Echoed the laugh of a pretty girl.

When winter comes,
   it is then I go
To a star-crowned hill
   that I used to know,
To dream of the wealth
   of peace and cheer
That was shaped by
   the snows of yesteryear.

And I oft' return
   to a lovely lane,
Where frost etched
   sparkling windowpanes
With charming scenes
   of the rare delight
That enthralled my heart
   of a winter's night.

Brian F. King

Wanderlust

I'm dancing to a minor strain
Where pale moonflowers sway;
A temple bell's deep old refrain
Calls from far Mandalay.

I'm savoring a spicy wind
From islands of the East;
On sunset through the tamarind
My avid eyes can feast.

I'm gathering exotic shells
From South Sea Island sands—
(But I'm really rolling cookie dough
With flour on my hands.)

Ruth B. Field

They think because I sew and bake
And sweep a white pine floor,
I never think of winding roads
Somewhere beyond my door!
They think me deaf to messages
Of winds in trees that bend
And sway in sheer abandonment,
While all I do is mend!

'Tis true, my body dwells at home
While a white shoreline calls
The roving heart and soul of me
Beyond these humble walls!
And so I sing and bake my bread
And baste my narrow seams,
But while I put my loaves in pans
My heart is light with dreams!

Author Unknown

Feeding the Birds

Hang this feeder beside the house,
And birds from field and stream
Will warble their magic music
And serenade your dreams.

Your dawns will be filled with melody,
From spring into golden fall,
And even in winter, some bright-eyed friends
Will pay you a social call.

Dan A. Hoover

The ground is frozen
And trees are bare.
Come one—come all
To taste my fare.

Sparrows, squirrels,
Ducks, and crows
Come to feast
On seeds and rolls.

In return,
Your antic chatter
Brings me gladness,
Warmth, and laughter.

L.L. Steinmiller

Photo Opposite
FEEDING THE DUCKS
H. Armstrong Roberts

The Turn of the Year

I'm always glad when winter's turned
The corner of the year,
When we can look ahead a bit
And know that spring is near.
Can feel a tugging at your heart,
To think of sprouting grain,
When the days are getting longer
And the sun is warm again.

When Mother starts to figure up
The hens she's going to set,
And looks at the seed catalogs
To find the seeds she'll get.
And Dad brings bits of harness in
To oil them up and sew,
And plants a hundred grains of wheat
To see how much will grow.

And when you're watering up the stock
And lead them from the well,
They lay their faces to the wind
And sort of sniff and smell,
And shake their heads and fluff their manes
And prance a step or two,
With little squeals of sheer delight—
You know how horses do.

The hens are dusting in the sun
Before the stable door,
Or scratching 'round among the feed
That's scattered on the floor.
The sunrise has a softer look,
A sort of hazy blue,
And in the fields so deep with snow
The sod is showing through.

For spring will come with faith and hope,
With sun and wind and rain,
The mirage still will paint her seas
Upon the lonely plain.
New wheat will deck a thousand fields,
New birds will nest and sing,
And we can hope, when winter's turned
The corner of the spring.

Edna Jaques

Photo Overleaf
EARLY SPRING HYACINTHS
H. Armstrong Roberts

TRAVEL

"A lavish tribute to the Southwest."

— New York Times Book Review

This unique, gorgeous compilation of word and image unites four crystalline essays by Tony Hillerman, some never before published, and thirty-six color photos by two award-winning photographers. "New Mexico" is a beautifully evoked homage to Hillerman's adoptive home state, while "Rio Grande" follows the course of the great river from its origins in the Continental Divide to its mouth on the Gulf of Mexico. "A Canyon, an Egret and a Book" vividly shows how Hillerman draws inspiration for his novels from the landscape, and "Places for Spirits, Places for Ghosts" tours the sites held most sacred by the Navajos and other tribes. Each essay is accompanied by superb full-color photos that blend with Hillerman's prose to evoke the Southwest's stark beauty.

Hillerman fans and lovers of the Southwestern landscape will find this beautiful volume a delight.

TONY HILLERMAN has achieved worldwide fame for his mysteries set in and around the Navajo Reservations, most recently Sacred Clowns and Coyote Waits. His nonfiction includes the classic The Great Taos Bank Robbery and Hillerman Country. He lives in Albuquerque, New Mexico.

HarperPerennial
A Division of HarperCollinsPublishers

Cover design by Suzanne Noli
Cover Photograph © 1993 by David Muench

| USA | $16.00 |
| CANADA | $22.50 |

ISBN 0-06-097558-X

51600>

9 780060 975586